REASON
AND
RATIONALITY

REASON
AND
RATIONALITY

Jon Elster

Translated by Steven Rendall

PRINCETON UNIVERSITY PRESS

Princeton & Oxford

Published by Princeton University Press, 41 William Street
Princeton, New Jersey 08540
In the United Kingdom: Princeton University Press,
6 Oxford Street, Woodstock, Oxfordshire OX20 1TW

LIBRARY OF CONGRESS CATALOGING-IN-PUBLICATION DATA

Elster, Jon, 1940–
[Raison et raisons. English]
Reason and rationality / Jon Elster ; translated by Steven
Rendall.
p.   cm.
Includes bibliographical references.
ISBN 978-0-691-13900-5 (hardcover : alk. paper)
1. Practical reason.   2. Rational choice theory.
3. Philosophy and social sciences.   I. Title.
BC177.E4713 2009
128'.33—dc22   2008029705

British Library Cataloging-in-Publication Data is available

This book has been composed in Adobe Garamond and
Goudy Trajan

Printed on acid-free paper.∞

press.princeton.edu

Printed in the United States of America

1 3 5 7 9 10 8 6 4 2

❧ CONTENTS ❧

REASON
AND
RATIONALITY

In analytical approaches to human behaviors, the same Latin word, *ratio,* is at the root of two intellectual traditions that are at once very different and interconnected.

On the one hand, there is the tradition that opposes reason to the passions and, more recently, to interests. Seneca's treatise *On Anger,* for instance, is organized around the opposition between reason and passion, whereas the French moralists of the seventeenth century added the notion of self-interest. La Bruyère, in a famous passage, summed up their mutual relationships this way: "Nothing is easier for passion than to overcome reason, but its greatest triumph is to conquer a man's own interest."[1] The idea of reason is intimately connected to that of the common good.

On the other hand, there is the still more recent idea of rational choice, which is opposed to the diverse forms of irrationality. The rational actor is one who acts for sufficient reasons. These reasons are the beliefs and desires in light of which the action appears to be appropriate in a sense that I shall discuss at length. The idea of rationality is often but wrongly related to that of the actor's private good or self-interest in

[1] La Bruyère (2007), p. 98.

the moralists' sense. Anyone who is pursuing the common good can—and even ought to—do so in a rational manner.

Acting in conformity with reason, in the singular, and acting for good reasons, in the plural, are two different things insofar as reason is objective, whereas reasons are subjective. From an external point of view, we can evaluate a policy as being in conformity with reason or not. From an internal point of view, one can evaluate an action as being rational or not.[2] From this difference it follows that only rationality can be used for explanatory ends. It is only insofar as the agent has made the demands of reason his own that the latter may give rise to, and possibly explain, specific behaviors. The

[2] For this distinction, see Williams (1981).

assessment of the actor and that of the observer need not coincide.

Although they are different, the two norms encounter a common obstacle, namely, the passions.[3] They also have a common com-

---

[3] Although it is quite classical, various objections to this opposition have recently been raised. Concerning the relationship between the emotions and rationality, see in particular Damasio (1994) according to whom individuals suffering from a brain lesion have both deficient rationality and a reduced ability to feel emotions. But it does not seem proven that this is a causal connection rather than a simple correlation. On the relationship between the emotions and reason, see especially Rudenfeld (2001), according to whom reason needs the help of passion in order to overcome self-interest. This was also Clermont-Tonnere's view in the Constituent Assembly of 1789: "Anarchy is a dreadful but necessary stage, and it is the only time when one can arrive at a new order of things. Uniform measures would not be taken in calm times" (*AP* 9:461). The night of August 4th has led some to draw the same conclusion. The debates of the Constituent Assembly nonetheless include ambiguities that seriously complicate matters; one has to agree with Toqueville, for

ponent, which is the idea of acting in accord with well-founded beliefs. Finally, they have in common the fact that they are the object of a certain deference on the part of the actor. The origin and nature of this deference are not the same, but in both cases it is a matter of deference with regard to a source of normativity.[4] The operation of mechanisms of deference is complex. For the moment, let it suffice to say that their effect is sometimes to subvert the object of deference.

It might be objected that comparing a principle concerning normative political

---

example, when he writes that "the night of August 4th [. . .] was the combined product, but in doses that cannot be determined with precision, of fear and enthusiasm" (2004b, p. 593).

[4] I borrow this phrase from Korsgaard (1996), who uses it, however, in a narrower sense.

philosophy with another that concerns the explanation of individual behavior is wrongheaded. One modest but sufficient reply to this objection would be to say that considering the usual confusions on this subject, conceptual clarification is worth pursuing for its own sake.

More ambitiously, I shall reply that clarification also has its place in political debate. Is it true, is it coherent, to say that the common good can be realized only through the pursuit of private goods? Is it true that the more rational actors are, the better reason's demands are met? Or must we see, inversely, the rationality of individuals as an obstacle to reason? Take, for example, the "voter's paradox," which results from the fact that the rational actor has no reason to vote.[5] In fact, the chance of having an influence on the outcome of the election is clearly less than the risk of dying in a traffic accident on the way to the polls. Moreover, those who are in the best position to understand the logic of this line of reasoning—in particular, professional economists—choose the cooperative strategy less often in the "prisoner's dilemma," of which voting is a classical example.[6]

Whereas the theory of rational choice has been elaborated and developed with great precision, the same cannot be said of the idea of reason. The conception that I am going to propose is not based on a ca-

[5] See Blais (2000).
[6] Frank, Gilovich, and Regan (1993).

nonical definition, because there is none. It represents a personal—but, I hope, not too idiosyncratic—synthesis of classical texts.

Let us begin with a remark of La Bruyère's: "To think only of oneself and of the present time is a source of error in politics."[7] To correct this error, we have to consider both other people and the future. More precisely, we must substitute an impartial attitude for the partial perspectives constituted by egoism and myopia.

The idea that reason requires an impartial treatment of individuals corresponds to well-known principles. To resolve the questions of distributive justice, Leibniz proposes the following maxim: "Put your-

[7] La Bruyère (2007), p. 358.

self in the place of everyone."[8] In recent theories, this amounts to saying that the choice of a just organization of society must take place behind a "veil of ignorance," an idea that can be interpreted in several ways.[9] For utilitarianism, each individual must count as one, and none as more than one. For John Rawls, we have to choose the form of society that favors the least advantaged, whoever they might be. Another impartial idea is that of universal rights, embodied in the two declarations of 1776 and 1789.

Less emphasis has been put on the idea, which is just as important, that reason requires impartial treatment of temporal instants. In itself, no date can be accorded

[8] See Elster (1975), pp. 127–30.
[9] See, for example, Fleurbaey (1996).

special privilege. Let us take first an absurd example:[10] always preferring goods that come on Thursdays to those that come on Wednesdays, solely because of a preference for that particular day of the week. As we shall see, this is not contrary to the principles of rational choice, but it is certainly contrary to reason. The simple preference for Thursdays is a reason, but reason also demands the reason for that reason. And obviously there is none.

Let us now take a less absurd example: preferring to receive a hundred dollars today rather than two hundred dollars a year from now. This preference is not necessarily contrary to reason. If my life expectancy is less than a year, it is perfectly well

[10] Borrowed from Parfit (1984), pp. 124–25.

founded. If on the other hand it results simply from the fact that our "telescopic faculty" is deficient, as economists say, it is contrary to reason. From an objective point of view, a person who takes into account the long-term consequences of present actions has a better chance of leading a long and happy life than one who considers only immediate effects. We shall see that this fact has no relevance from a subjective point of view.

We can consider in this perspective the idea of "interest properly understood" such as it is used by Tocqueville, for example. Once again, in view of the absence of explicit definitions in classical authors, we must attempt a synthesis of their ideas. It seems to me that interest properly understood includes at least two components.

On the one hand, it considers the long-term consequences of action. In technical language, it corresponds to a low rate of discounting of the future. On the other hand, it is based on well-founded beliefs, in a sense that I shall explain later.

Characterized in this way, interest properly understood is an amalgam of objective and subjective elements. An entirely objective conception would substitute true beliefs for well-founded beliefs. But it is impossible to make political decisions dependent on the possession of truth. At most we can demand that they be founded on rational beliefs, that is, beliefs that result from unbiased processing of an optimal quantity of information, to sum up a complex idea that will be developed in a moment. Let it suffice here to say that since the optimum quantity of information depends on the discount rate, the objective constraints that influence this rate also introduce an objective element into the optimum.

In this reconstruction, the idea of reason comprises three elements: impartiality with regard to persons, temporal impartiality, and rational or well-founded beliefs. No doubt we should add goodwill, in order to exclude impartial malice. Sometimes we encounter the suggestion that the first element (impartiality with regard to persons) is redundant, since it follows from the second (temporal impartiality). From Descartes's correspondence with Princess Elisabeth to the theory of repeated games, it has often been observed that farsighted egoism is capable of mimicking altruism.[11] However, the conditions under which one can count on the operation of this invisible hand are relatively restrictive.

The theory of rational choice is first of all normative, and only secondarily explanatory.[12] It begins by stating how agents should act in order to realize their goals, and then proposes to explain their actions on the hypothesis that they actually behave in that manner (see fig. 1).

[11] On this point, I refer the reader to Elster (2006a).
[12] Economists who believe that rationality is mere coherence would deny this claim. For convincing refutations of their view, see Sen (1973) and Hausman (1990).

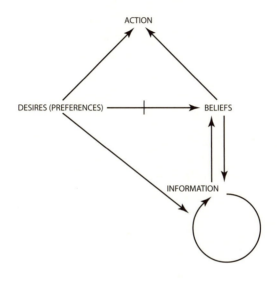

FIGURE I

Desires and beliefs are reasons for action. A rational actor chooses the action that will realize his desire as well as possible, given his beliefs and the totality of his other desires. These are sufficient reasons, which determine in a unique manner what must be done. I shall return to the possibility of non-uniqueness, but for the moment I limit myself to the ideal case.

Desires include both preferences that might be called substantial, such as preferring apples to oranges, and formal preferences, such as one's attitude toward risk and the future. An individual may prefer the certitude of having 100 dollars to a lottery that offers equal chances of winning 90 or 120 dollars. He may also prefer 100 dollars today to 110 tomorrow. Under precise and quite reasonable conditions, these preferences can be represented as a *utility function* that assigns each option a numerical value. This will then allow us to say that the rational agent maximizes his utility.

This expression does not imply egoism, as is sometimes said. Any coherent desire, whether egoistic, altruistic, or malicious, is compatible with the demands of rationality. Only incoherent desires are excluded, such as the wish that everyone earn more than average or the desire to be present at one's own funeral in order to hear one's eulogy, like Tom Sawyer and Huckleberry Finn. For Sartre, the latter contradiction, the desire to be both in-itself and for-itself, defines human existence. While this desire can no doubt give rise to actions, they do not fall within the domain of the rational.

A desire may also exhibit pragmatic incoherence, in the sense that the means for realizing the desired state prevent it from being realized. As Paul Veyne has written, "only an expression that is not trying to produce an effect produces one."[13] But before Veyne, there was already Proust: "Each great artist seems to be the citizen of an unknown homeland which he has forgotten [. . .] It is not that musicians can remember this lost homeland, but each always remains unconsciously in tune with it; he is overcome with joy when he sings the songs of his country, he may sometimes betray it for the sake of glory, but when he seeks glory in this way he moves further away from it,

[13] Veyne (1976), p. 679; see also my study of this book in Elster (1990), chap. 1.

and only finds it when he turns his back on it."[14]

We could analyze in the same way fruitless attempts to overcome, by a mere effort of the will, insomnia, sexual impotence, or stuttering. This does not exclude the possibility of realizing the desired states in an indirect way, as is shown by the existence of sleeping pills and Viagra. To remain within the Sartrean tradition, we could also mention paradoxical injunctions such as "be spontaneous."[15] In a religious register, theologies often teach that an action undertaken with the sole purpose of gaining access to Paradise cannot provide that

[14] Proust (2003b), pp. 235–36; see also, in the same vein, p. 342.
[15] See, especially, Watzlawick (1978).

access.[16] We might add that from the moral point of view, certain French Nazi collaborators' efforts to redeem themselves in 1944 through acts of resistance carried out solely to that end should not have caused the charges against them to be dismissed, as they sometimes did.[17]

Desires may also be incoherent in a third sense, if their internal structure subverts their realization. To illustrate this idea, let us take the example of intertemporal choice.[18] In a general way, we can represent the present value of a future good as a function of the time separating the present from this future. In the classical conception, an

[16] See, for example, Elster (2004b) on suicide attacks carried out in the hope of achieving personal salvation.

[17] See Elster (2006b) for examples and analyses; also Chauvy (2003).

[18] See Loewenstein and Elster (1992).

exponential future discount is stipulated, which implies that the curves corresponding to two distinct future goods, one small and immediate, the other large and more remote, never intersect. According to more recent research, however, it seems that this discount typically takes a hyperbolic form. As the agent moves through time, a moment will arrive when the remote good that initially seemed to him more desirable will cease to be so, leading him to choose the lesser but closer good (see fig. 2).

The beliefs involved in this calculation concern either particular facts or causal relationships. On the one hand, the agent can choose only among the options that he thinks are available to him. The objective existence of an option superior to those he is aware of cannot influence his action. On

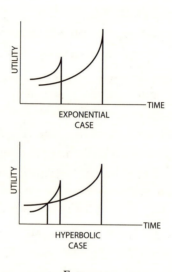

FIGURE 2

the other hand, the agent chooses among the options of which he is aware according to the possible consequences he attributes to them and his estimate of the probability that they will occur. Thus the utility of the options is deduced from the utility of the consequences, weighted by their probability and reduced to a present value by the agent's discount rate.

For action to be rational, the beliefs on which it is based must themselves be well founded. In turn, this requirement is divided into two parts. On the one hand, the beliefs must be unbiased with respect to the information the agent possesses; on the other hand, he must gather an optimal amount of information.

Even though an agent may make errors, he must not do so systematically. Since biases are countless, it would be desirable to be able to propose a positive definition, but no one has succeeded in offering one. That is because the formulation of beliefs frequently includes an irreducible element of *judgment* or subjective appreciation of the relative importance of the diverse, often heterogeneous bits of information that are at the agent's disposal. Thus it has been said that the former head of the Federal Reserve Bank, Alan Greenspan, had an almost intuitive knowledge of the markets unequaled by any economic theoretician.[19]

Biases are either "hot" (that is, produced by the agent's motivational system) or "cold" (more similar to optical illusions).

---

[19] Paul Krugman, *New York Times*, October 28, 2005. It should be said that Krugman's assessment of Greenspan has changed since that time.

The former, which we may call "motivated beliefs" and which are indicated by the barred arrow in figure 1, have always been known. They are summed up in numerous sayings such as La Fontaine's observation, "Everyone finds it easy to believe what he fears and what he desires." The tendency to believe what one fears shows that motivated beliefs do not necessarily assume the form of "taking one's desires for realities." Consider, for instance, two jealous husbands like M. de Rênal and Othello, the former believing what he desires and the latter believing what he fears,[20] neither with any justification in the facts.

[20] M. de Rênal is a character in Stendhal's novel *The Red and the Black*. For one of the rare discussions of the subject that takes into account both "countermotivated" beliefs and motivated beliefs, see Mele (2001).

Cold biases also have a long history. Here, for example, is how Montaigne explains the errors in reasoning that lead people to believe in the accuracy of divinations: "That explains the reply made by Diagoras, surnamed the Atheist, when he was in Samothrace: he was shown many vows and votive portraits from those who have survived shipwrecks and was then asked, 'You, there, who think that the gods are indifferent to human affairs, what have you to say about so many men saved by their grace?'— 'It is like this', he replied, 'there are no portraits here of those who stayed and drowned—and they are more numerous!' "[21] Modern psychology has identified a large number of similar errors that, for

[21] Montaigne (1991), p. 440.

obvious reasons, lend themselves better to experimentation than do hot errors.

For a rational actor, the information he uses to shape his beliefs is a variable rather than a given. Before deciding how to act, he has to make a preliminary decision concerning the quantity of resources he is prepared to invest in looking for the relevant facts. A general must not attack before he has surveyed the terrain, or a surgeon operate before he has examined the patient. However, they must not delay too long, for then they may be surprised by the enemy's attack or flight, or by the patient's death. Thus there exists in principle an optimal investment that depends on the agent's preferences as well as on his beliefs regarding the expected costs and benefits. In buying a car, for example, a rational agent who attaches little importance to the distant future is not going to make a great effort to compare the durability of various models. Neither is he going to consult his physician to find out more about the risks that may be involved in consuming bacon, alcohol, or cigarettes.

To emphasize the radically subjective nature of the notion of rationality that I have just laid out, let us take a hypothetical example. Suppose a person is suffering—and that is the right word—from a high discount rate, that is, he attaches very little importance to the long-term consequences of his actions. As a result of his lack of foresight, his finances and his health are deteriorating. Then a remedy for his problem is proposed to him: a pill that will make him attach more importance to the future. Will he take it? For a rational person, the answer must be in the negative. All the actions that would be induced by the pill are already in his repertory. If he does not choose them, that is because he does not desire to carry them out. Therefore he does not desire to make the choice that would make him carry them out.

The premise of this statement is what one might call the *principle of non-indirection*. I call "indirection" an indirect operation that makes it possible to arrive at a certain result through two successive actions, the first of which serves only to make the second possible. For instance, to find my keys, I must first find my glasses. In this case, I would have no objection to finding my keys without putting my glasses on; it's simply that I can't do it. In the case of the pill, the situation is the inverse: I could begin right now to take care of my finances and my health, only I don't want to. The principle of non-indirection states that a rational agent will refuse to do in two steps what he would not do in one step, which does not exclude indirect operations for ends that he *cannot* realize in a single action.

This principle is not limited to rational actions. Let us consider another hypothetical action. I've lost my head and gotten involved in an adulterous affair. My wife knows nothing about it and, let us suppose, never will. I nonetheless have a very strong feeling of guilt that leads me to break off the affair. Now let us suppose that a friend offers me a pill that will eliminate this feeling and allow me to continue my affair with a clear conscience. The principle of non-indirection implies that I must refuse the pill, because I would feel just as guilty taking it as I would by continuing the affair. My friend sees this differently: he thinks I will be happier once I've taken the pill. Once I've taken it, I myself will be happy I took it. But that does not in any way affect the fact that from my point of view *ex ante* I must refuse. If this conclusion is accepted, then we must reject the idea according to which emotions intervene in decisions only by virtue of the pleasures or pains associated with them.[22] It is entirely rational to take, before going to a party, a pill that will spare me a hangover

[22] This idea is found especially in the works of Gary Becker; see Elster (1999), chap. 4, for a critical discussion.

the next morning; but a feeling of guilt is not the same thing as a headache.

The principle of non-indirection thus expresses a broader idea of coherence that includes the emotional as well as the rational. That said, violations of the principle are quite frequent, as in the case of German or Norwegian employees who are too proud to accept public subsidies for their salaries, but who accept their companies' being allowed to pay a lower electricity rate for the sole purpose of maintaining employment.[23] Another example of the violation of this principle: at the Constitutional Convention held in Philadelphia in 1787, in order to appease those who were opposed to the idea of counting slaves in determining the

[23] See Schlicht (1984) and Serck-Hanssen (1971).

basis for electoral representation, James Wilson proposed to include them in the basis for taxation and then to make the latter the basis for representation.[24]

One might also express the subjectivity of rational choice by saying that the eye cannot see beyond its own horizon. In the keys example, for instance, let us substitute glasses for the lost keys. One cannot put on one's glasses in order to find them. Another metaphor: the rational agent is caught in the trap of his desires and beliefs. We have just seen in what sense that may be true for the attitude toward the future. To show that the idea is also applicable to beliefs, we can define a *belief-trap* by the fact that the anticipated costs of verifying it are so

[24] Farrand (1966), 1:561.

elevated that a rational agent would refrain from doing so.[25] In Poland, until recently many people combated their alcoholism by having the substance disulfiram implanted under their skins.[26] Taken orally, disulfiram's only effect is to produce violent nausea if one drinks alcohol; in its subcutaneous form it was supposed to cause death if alcohol were consumed. In reality, the substance has no effect at all when it is implanted.[27] But so long as people believed that it did, it was rational on their part not to try to find out whether this was in fact the case.

The theory of rational actions assumes

[25] Mackie (1996).
[26] Osiatynski (1997).
[27] Johnsen and Mørland (1992).

the agents' desires and preferences as a fixed given. In figure 1, no arrow points to desires. In the Humean tradition, desires are the first causes of action. One does not choose one's desires. There are, of course, examples that run counter to this proposition. People may undergo psychotherapy to reduce the force of certain desires if they find it impossible to resist them. However, this case presupposes that the agent is irrational, because he is a victim of the weakness of his will. In choosing the action that will realize his desire, he does not take into account the totality of his desires. For a rational actor, the problem of choosing his desires does not arise. To desire to have a certain desire is already to have it. Wanting to be motivated by the long-term consequences of action is already to have that motivation.[28]

There are gaps in the theory of rational action, since it is sometimes incapable of determining a specific action that would result from the agent's beliefs and desires. From the point of view of the sociology of science, it is perhaps the promise of uniqueness that explains to a great extent the theory's enormous success. To be sure, it is an elementary mathematical fact that a "well-behaved" function defined over a "well-behaved" set reaches its maximum at a specific value of the independent variable. The determination of the consumer's choice as the point of tangency between the line representing the budgetary constraint and an

---

[28] The question is more complicated, however; see Elster (2007).

indifference curve offers a classical illustration of this point. Like the Newtonian equations, the model of the rational agent thus seems to incarnate the scientific ideal of predictive uniqueness.

However, we have long known that in physics the n-body problem has, in general, no analytical solution. In a vaguely similar manner—this is only a pedagogical comparison—there are situations in which the interaction of n agents has no single optimal solution or equilibrium. Here I do not intend to enter into this aspect of game theory. I prefer to emphasize another source of the non-uniqueness of rational action, namely, the acquisition of information.

Suppose you have gone to gather wild strawberries, which are as rare and as difficult to find as they are delicious.[29] You're on vacation in a region you don't know well, and you have hardly any pre-conceived ideas concerning the distribution of the secret and magic places that give their name to Bergman's famous film, *Smultronstället* (poorly translated into English as *Wild Strawberries*). You look around the fields, more or less at random, knowing that they will all give you at least a few scattered berries, but also that some of them might allow you to fill your basket in a single hour. The question that arises is this: when do you stop looking and start picking, as best you can?

Since you have only a single day, you know you have to stop looking before night-

[29] Example borrowed from Johansen (1977), p. 144; see also Winter (1964), p. 262.

fall. However, you also know that beginning to pick in the first field you come across is generally not the optimal strategy, unless, of course, it turns out to be one of the magic places, a possibility that is represented by the loop in figure 1. Between this maximum and this minimum of investment, there is no doubt an objective optimum, but how can it be determined? Often, the general and the physician whom I mentioned earlier find themselves in the same situation. Between the minimum and the maximum of time at their disposal for collecting information, there is an indeterminate zone that may be larger or smaller depending on the case, but which is often considerable. Even if good judgment makes it possible to form a rational belief on the basis of a given quantity of information, it is sometimes incapable of determining the optimal quantity.

The theory of rational action may therefore fail, because it is unable to produce *unique* prescriptions and predictions. It may also fail if the agents' behavior does not conform to predictions, whether these are unique or not; that is, if the agents are irrational. There are multiple sources of irrationality, hot or cold. Here, I would like to mention above all the role of the emotions, which are capable of acting on each of the four poles of action (see fig. 3).

Weakness of the will—acting against the totality of one's desires under the influence of one of them—is often due to the fact that the dominant desire arises from a strong emotion. As Ovid's Medea says when she is about to kill her children in

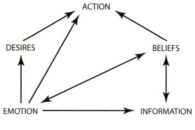

FIGURE 3

order to take revenge on their father, who deceived and abandoned her, "I see the good and approve it; and I follow the bad."

Through another mechanism, the emotions produce a temporary inversion or reversal of preferences. A simple illustration is provided by desertion in the face of danger. One may well have a firm intention to stand fast against enemy attack, abandon this intention under the shock of terror, and then bitterly regret having done so. In the army, this regret sometimes leads deserters to return to the ranks. Thus in the American Civil War, 10 percent of the two hundred thousand men who deserted from the Union army voluntarily returned to it.[30]

[30] Costa and Kahn (2007).

Just as the emotions arise from beliefs, they also influence them in turn. On the one hand, Stendhal tells us, "It only needs a very small quantity of hope to beget love. [. . .] From the moment he falls in love even the wisest man no longer sees anything *as it really is*. [. . .] He no longer admits an element of chance in things and loses his sense of the probable; judging by its effect on his happiness, whatever he imagines becomes reality."[31]

Finally, the *urgency* of the emotions induces a preference for immediate action over deferred action. I distinguish between urgency and impatience, the latter inducing a preference for an immediate reward over a deferred reward. Thus defined, urgency

[31] Stendhal (1957), chaps. 3 and 12.

produces a short circuit in the acquisition of information. Seneca praised Fabius for knowing how "to wait, temporize—all things of which an angry man is incapable." More generally, he says, "reason grants a hearing to both sides, then seeks to postpone action, even its own, in order that it may gain time to sift out the truth; but anger is precipitate."

That said, there are clearly dangerous situations where immediate action is required and where waiting would be disastrous. What is difficult is to distinguish justified prompt actions from panic reactions. After September 11, 2001, were the reactions of Western governments appropriate or excessive? Did they attenuate the danger or increase it? The question is not only whether there was sufficient deliberation, but also whether it was biased in the sense that one believes too easily what one fears.

I would now like to broaden the analysis by distinguishing between desires and motivations. Whereas desires bear directly on the action to be undertaken, motivations are more fundamental attitudes that give rise to desires. Thus the desire to punish someone who has offended you can be produced by self-interested calculation, by an emotion, or by an impartial principle of retributive justice. As I said at the outset and as this example suggests, I shall follow the moralists by distinguishing among three main motivations: reason, the passions, and self-interest.

I have already tried to explain what reason consists in. I will now interpret it as a motivation interiorized by the agent, in a somewhat indirect sense, as we shall see. I conceive passion in a broad sense that includes not only the emotions, but also madness, intoxication, and the appetites of drug addicts. Interest, finally, is understood in the sense of personal advantage, whether in material goods, power, prestige, or glory.

In any society, there is a normative hierarchy of motivations. One is praised for having performed a given action with this or that motivation, independently of the praise or blame attached to the action itself.

In ancient Greece, patriotism, the will to defend the City, was at the summit of the hierarchy; then came passionate revenge for a personal affront, then self-interest, sexual desire, and drunkenness. At the bottom of the scale were envy and *hubris* (the deliberate humiliation of others). In other societies, vengeance comes before patriotism; in still others, it is situated lower than self-interest on the scale of values.

According to Tocqueville, the Americans of his age inverted the order of reason and self-interest in the hierarchy:

> [Unlike Europe, where people] daily feign a readiness for sacrifice they no longer possess[,] Americans by contrast, are pleased to explain nearly all their actions in terms of self-interest properly

understood. They will obligingly demonstrate how enlightened love of themselves regularly leads them to help one another out and makes them ready and willing to sacrifice a portion of their time and wealth for the good of the state. On this point I believe that they often fail to do themselves justice. For one sometimes sees citizens of the United States, like citizens of other countries, yielding to the disinterested, spontaneous impulses that are part of man's nature. But Americans seldom admit that they give in to enthusiasms of this kind. They would rather do honor to their philosophy than to themselves.[32]

---

[32] Tocqueville (2004a), p. 611.

Recent studies suggest that this attitude persists in Western societies in various forms.[33] The question is complicated by the fact that the source of the disapproval of impartial or altruistic motivations is often the suspicion that the claimed disinterest is in fact no more than a pose. To avert this suspicion, even a person as angelic as the grandmother in Proust's novel always attributes what she does to "selfish motives."[34] Even if reason dominates self-interest in the hierarchy, self-interest takes precedence over the ostentatious affectation of reason. To quote Montaigne, "The more glittering the deed the more I subtract from its moral worth, because of the suspicion aroused in me that

[33] Miller (1999).
[34] Proust (2003a), p. 246.

it was exposed more for glitter than for goodness; goods displayed are already halfway to being sold."[35] We shall see that Montaigne could have been still more radical.

Let us assume the existence of a hierarchy of emotions, whatever it may be, and try to determine its effects. To win praise or avoid blame, it is in a rational agent's interest to make his motivation appear to be located at a level in the hierarchy more elevated than it is in fact. He may have an interest in the appearance of reason or in the appearance of emotion, as in societies where trying to find a rich wife is a motive that cannot be acknowledged. But simultaneously with this second-order motivation, he nonetheless retains the desire that is in-

[35] Montaigne (1991), pp. 1157–58.

spired by the first-order motivation; whence a potential conflict.

Hypocrisy involves deceiving others with regard to one's true motivations. Trials before the ancient Greek juries (*dikasters*) provide many examples of this. Thus accusers who feared that they might themselves be accused of being sycophants found it advantageous to pretend to be motivated by revenge rather than by their material self-interest.[36] In public debates, every self-interested proposal has to be presented as concerning the public interest. The great political parties, which have an interest in a majoritarian electoral system, generally defend it in the name of efficiency; the small parties, which have an interest in a

---

[36] Hansen (1991), p. 195.

proportional system, often justify the latter in the name of democracy. When there is a hierarchy internal to reason, social utility being subordinated, for instance, to property rights, proposals motivated by the former might be defended in the name of the latter. This was the case for the confiscation of the French clergy's property in October 1789.[37]

But the homage vice pays to virtue may also take the form of bad faith or self-deception. According to Jean Domat, "all the heart's deference to the mind consists in this: if it does not act on the basis of reason, it at least makes it appear that it is acting on the basis of reason."[38] Self-esteem may be a motive as important as the esteem of

[37] See, for instance, *AP* 9:639 ff., 649 ff.
[38] Domat (1992), p. 611.

others. In fact, the very act of renouncing the external audience is often applauded by the internal audience, and may be carried out for the sake of this applause rather than for its own sake. As La Rochefoucauld says, "Pridefulness always finds compensations, and even when it gives up vanity it loses nothing."[39] A charitable donation, even if it is made secretly, may be compensated by the strengthening of self-esteem that it produces. To that extent, Montaigne's suspicion is not radical enough.

Often, however, we use reason to *justify* interested actions. Even if my self-interest tells me not to give to charities, I want to retain the image of myself as a person who is not motivated solely by self-interest. I

[39] La Rochefoucauld (1982), maxim 33.

can satisfy both demands by adopting a principle of charity suited to the circumstances. If others give a great deal, I abstain from giving, telling myself that my contribution would add little.[40] If others give little, I can also abstain from giving, telling myself that fairness demands that I be generous only if others are being generous as well.[41] In both cases, I get to eat my cake and have it too. In a similar way, as La Rochefoucauld puts it, "A refusal of praise is a desire to be praised twice."[42]

The passions also often seek to wrap themselves in reason. As Seneca says, "reason wants to decide what is just; anger wants what it has decided to appear to be

[40] Margolis (1982).
[41] Sugden (1984).
[42] La Rochefoucauld (1982), maxim 149.

just."[43] In 1945, the French, like the Belgians, Norwegians, Danes, Hungarians, and Dutch, were torn between two motives: a passionate desire for vengeance, and the desire to respect legal principles and especially the principle of the nonretroactivity of the law. In many cases, in fact, the acts that people wanted to punish were not prohibited by the laws in force at the time they were committed.

The Hungarians, Danes, and Dutch overtly chose retroactivity. In France, Belgium, and Norway, retroactive laws were presented as if they were not retroactive. In France it was said that since the acts described as national indignities were political rather than criminal in nature, there

[43] Seneca, *On Anger*, 1.18.

was no violation of the principle "no law, no crime." This was merely a verbal sleight of hand, since the national degradation that punished these acts was a flagrant violation of another, equally important principle: "No law, no punishment."[44]

A passion may also seek to cover itself with a passion higher up in the hierarchy. As Plutarch notes, people often present the shameful passion of envy in the guise of anger or hatred.[45] For example, anti-Semitism often arises from envy transmuted into self-satisfied indignation. In another register, the Huguenots' iconoclasm was often motivated by a spirit of hatred and vengeance rather than by the love of God.

[44] For the observations in the last two paragraphs, see Elster (2004a), p. 237–40.

[45] Plutarch, *On Envy and Hatred*.

Although they have a very broad field of operation, these mechanisms are also subjected to major constraints. To be sure, their application is facilitated by the fact that agents have *two degrees of freedom* in harmonizing their motivations and desires. First, there are many conceptions of impartiality, some appealing to individual rights, others to the notion of fairness or to choice behind the veil of ignorance. In any given case, the implications for action may be extremely diverse, as we have just seen in the case of charity.

Second, every political decision of any importance is intertwined with questions of social causality on which very diverse positions can be defended with a certain degree of plausibility. Whether it is a question of the effects of the minimum wage, unemployment benefits, or tax rates, we see professors of economics defending entirely opposed ideas. Thus an agent would have to be either very inept or very unfortunate not to be able to find some combination of normative principles and causal chains that would allow him to present his passion or his particular interest in an impartial light.

However, these mechanisms are subject to two constraints that make their application less easy. First, there is a constraint of consistency: once the agent has adopted a certain normative principle or a certain causal theory, he cannot abandon it, even if it no longer allows him to satisfy his desires. Having adopted a principle of fairness to justify my parsimonious contributions to charity, I am obliged to continue to adhere to it even if others begin to give a great deal, since otherwise I would appear to myself as moved solely by my self-interest, which is precisely the appearance I wanted to avoid. It is easier to enter a state through bad faith than to escape from it by the same mechanism.

Second, there is what might be called a constraint of imperfection, which is connected with the fact that the coincidence between the professed motivation and the desire must not be too blatant. In order to conceal one's true motivations from the external or the internal audience, one must often act to some extent against one's desires. Let us suppose that I want to make people believe that a marriage proposal is motivated by love rather than by money. To maintain the illusion, I must not choose a person whose sole quality is the possession of a large fortune, even if it is solely the latter that dictates my preference.

Nonetheless, confronted by an internal or external audience that carries hermeneutic suspicion very far, the only way to convince is sometimes to renounce one's desires. Pascal notes that "our own interest is [a] wonderful instrument for blinding us agreeably. The fairest man in the world is not allowed to be judge in his own case. I know of men who, to avoid the danger of partiality in their own favor, have leaned over to the opposite extreme of injustice. The surest way to lose a perfectly just case was to get close relatives to recommend it to them."[46] Sometimes only an attitude contrary to one's self-interest

[46] Pascal (1995), pensée 44.

is capable of producing the appearance of impartiality.

This deference to reason, to adopt Jean Domat's expression, has its counterpart in a certain deference with regard to rationality. Rationality is a norm, for reasons that have to do with logic rather than with a social hierarchy of values. If one wants to satisfy a desire, one will inevitably want to do so at the minimum cost and avoiding useless expense. Any possible counterexample would be tantamount to a richer specification of his initial desire. That is why rationality, unlike impartiality, is a transhistorical and transcultural factor. The many attempts to deduce the latter from the former are doomed to failure.

The norm of rationality is at the heart of philosophical anthropology, whereas the norm of impartiality belongs to empirical anthropology. There are societies in which the neglect or violation of impartial values does not prompt social sanctions. That does not mean that these societies are not familiar with altruistic or disinterested behaviors, but only, as Tocqueville said about the Americans of his time, that these behaviors are presented as the result of interest properly understood. The ability of foresightful egoism to mimic altruism also allows altruism to make itself appear egoistic.

Let us recall that the norm of impartiality, as a social norm, bears on the motivation of an action rather than on the action itself. That said, the norm may also modify action, as is immediately implied by the constraints of consistency and imperfection. From the social point of view, the effect of these constraints is often benign. We can speak not only of the civilizing power of hypocrisy, but also of the civilizing power of bad faith. However, the norm of impartiality also has a *strategic* use whose effect is more ambiguous.[47] Even in contexts where interested motivations are permitted, as in wage bargaining, the parties often appeal to the principles of equity or equality. Since giving up a principle constitutes a greater concession than giving up an interest, and thus calls for a greater counterconcession, it is to the advantage of all parties to present themselves as not being moved by

[47] On this point, see Elster (1995), with examples taken from the debates at the American Constitutional Congress (1787) and the French Constitutional Assembly (1789).

self-interest alone. If this behavior is generalized, agreement may prove impossible.[48] The appeal to reason subverts reason.

In a similar way, but through a different mechanism, the appeal to rationality may subvert rationality. The ideal of rational decision is to act in accord with sufficient reasons, in the light of which a unique, optimal solution emerges. There are, however, cases in which the search for the optimal action is not worth the trouble, and in which the rational actor would adopt a different procedure, such as following tradition or deciding to flip a coin. We can in fact define *hyperrationality* as the search for the action that would have been optimal if one ignored the costs of the search itself.[49]

[48] Elster (1989a), chap. 6.
[49] The best analyses remain those of Neurath (1913).

The costs of making a decision fall into three categories. First, there is the direct cost, which depends on the investment in the acquisition of information. If one goes from store to store to buy a given product as cheaply as possible, one has to take into account the cost of the taxi or the subway ticket. Then there is the opportunity cost, which is the value of the best alternative use of the time devoted to the collection of information. Even if the price of a subway ticket is lower than the expected gross benefit of buying at the lowest price, the half-hour trip could have been devoted to activities that have more value for the agent than the net benefit. Finally, there is the cost of the by-products of the decision process.

Neglect of the first two costs can be

observed in the behavior of vacationers in Roussillon. Many of them go to Spain by car to buy cigarettes at low prices, as if gasoline and time cost them nothing, not to mention the lines in the autoroute restaurants where they wait half an hour for a (mediocre) meal that they need after spending three hours in a traffic jam. When they get back, they can of course congratulate themselves on having saved money, but at an absurd price.[50]

Neglect of the third type of cost may have more important effects, as when the right to custody of children is assigned after a divorce.[51] In most Western countries, the law says that in case of disagreement between the parents, custody must be deter-

[50] *L'Indépendant* (Perpignan), August 13, 2005, p. 2.
[51] An example developed in Elster (1989b), chap. 3.

mined by "the best interests of the child"; that is, custody should be assigned to the parent best suited to promote the child's welfare. However, experience abundantly shows that juridico-psychological determination of the relative suitability of the parents is a process that is highly painful and harmful for the very child whose interests it is supposed to protect. The child's interest would probably be better respected by the traditional assumption in favor of the mother, or even—why not?—by drawing lots.

Modern Western societies are imbued with hyperrationality. It is in this sense, and in this sense only, that one may speak of rationality, or rather of its abuse, as a specifically Western or modern phenomenon. In this respect, the search for optimal solutions has been described as iatrogenic.[52] To a certain extent, one might say that "less is more."

&

What, finally, are the functions of reason and rationality in human behaviors? They are the functions, respectively, of the prince's tutor and his councilor. The tutor teaches the prince to promote the public good in the long term. The councilor tells him how to act in order to achieve his goals, whatever they might be, in the most efficient way. It is not incumbent upon the councilor to impose the demands of reason; but if the tutor has done his job well, the prince will make them his own.

[52] Wiener (1998).

◆ WORKS CITED ◆

AP = *Archives Parlementaires*. Première Série. Paris, 1875–88.

Blais, A. 2000. *To Vote or Not to Vote: The Merits and Limits of Rational Choice Theory*. University of Pittsburgh Press.

Chauvy, G. 2003. *Les acquittés de Vichy*. Paris: Perrin.

Costa, D., and M. Kahn. 2007. "Deserters, Social Norms, and Migration." *Journal of Law and Economics* 50:323–53.

Damasio, A. 1994. *Descartes's Error*. New York: Putnam.

Domat, J. 1992. "Pensées." In *Moralistes du XVIIᵉ siècle*, edited by J. Lafond. Paris: Robert Laffont.

Elster, J. 1975. *Leibniz et la formation de l'esprit capitaliste*. Paris: Aubier-Montaigne.

————. 1989a. *The Cement of Society*. Cambridge University Press.

————. 1989b. *Solomonic Judgements*. Cambridge University Press.

————. 1990. *Psychologie politique*. Paris: Éditions de Minuit.

————. 1995. "Strategic Uses of Argument." In *Barriers to the Negotiated Resolution of Conflict*, edited by K. Arrow et al. New York: Norton.

————. 1999. *Alchemies of the Mind*. Cambridge University Press.

————. 2004a. *Closing the Books: Transitional Justice in Historical Perspective*. Cambridge University Press.

————. 2004b. "Motivations and Beliefs in Suicide Missions." In *Making Sense of Suicide Missions*, edited by D. Gambetta. Oxford University Press.

———. 2006a. "Altruistic Behavior and Altruistic Motivations." In *The Economics of Giving, Altruism and Reciprocity*, edited by S.-C. Kolm and J.-M. Ythie, vol. 1. Amsterdam: Elsevier.

———. 2006b. "Redemption for Wrongdoing." *Journal of Conflict Resolution* 50:324–38.

———. 2007. *Agir contre soi*. Paris: Editions Odile Jacob.

Farrand, M. 1966. *Records of the Federal Convention*. New Haven, CT: Yale University Press.

Fleurbaey, M. 1996. *Théories économiques de la justice*. Paris: Economica.

Frank, R., T. Gilovich, and D. Regan. 1993. "Does Studying Economics Inhibit Cooperation?" *Journal of Economic Perspectives* 7:159–71.

Hansen, M. H. 1991. *The Athenian Democracy in the Age of Demosthenes.* Oxford: Blackwell.

Hausman, D. 1990. "Revealed Preference, Belief, and Game Theory." *Economics and Philosophy* 16:99–115.

Johansen, L. 1977. *Lectures on Macroeconomic Planning.* Amsterdam: North-Holland.

Johnsen, J., and J. Mørland. 1992. "Depot Preparations of Disulfiram: Experimental and Clinical Results." *Acta Psychiatrica Scandinavica* 86:27–30.

Korsgaard, C. 1996. *Sources of Normativity.* Cambridge University Press.

La Bruyère. 2007. *The Characters.* Translated by H. van Laun. Whitefish, MT: Kessinger Publishing.

La Rochefoucauld. 1982. *Maxims.* Translated

by Leonard Tancock. London: Penguin, 1982.

Loewenstein, G., and J. Elster, eds. 1992. *Choice over Time*. New York: Russell Sage.

Mackie, G. 1996. "Ending Footbinding and Infibulation: A Convention Account." *American Sociological Review* 61:999–1017.

Margolis, H. 1982. *Selfishness, Altruism, and Rationality*. Cambridge University Press.

Mele, A. 2001. *Self-Deception Unmasked*. Princeton University Press.

Miller, D. 1999. "The Norm of Self-Interest." *American Psychologist* 54:1053–60.

Montaigne, Michel de. 1991. *The Essays of Michel de Montaigne*. Translated by M. A. Screech. London: Allen Lane.

Neurath, O. 1913. "Die Verirrten des Cartesius und das Auxiliarmotiv. Zur Psychologie des Entschlusses." *Jahrbuch der Philosophischen*

Gesellschaft an der Universität Wien. Leipzig: Johann Ambrosius Barth.

Osiatynski, W. 1997. *Alcoholism: Sin or Disease?* Warsaw: Fondation Stefan Batory.

Parfit, D. 1984. *Reasons and Persons*. Oxford University Press.

Pascal, B. *Pensées*. Translated by A. J. Krailsheimer. London: Penguin, 1995.

Proust, M. 2003a. *In the Shadow of Young Girls in Flower*. London: Penguin Classics.

———. 2003b. *The Prisoner and The Fugitive*. London: Penguin Classics.

Rudenfeld, J. 2001. *Freedom and Time*. New Haven, CT: Yale University Press.

Schlicht, E. 1984. "Die emotive und die kognitive Gerechtigkeits-auffassung." *Ökonomie und Gesellschaft* 2:141–54.

Sen, A. 1973. "Behaviour and the Concept of Preference." *Economica* 40:241–59.

Serck-Hanssen, J. 1971. "Subsidiering av kapital i utbyggingsområdene." *Statsøkonomisk Tidsskrift* 84:140–61.

Stendhal. 1957. *On Love.* Translated by G. and S. Sale. London: Penguin.

Sugden, R. 1984. "Reciprocity: The Supply of Public Goods through Voluntary Contributions." *Economic Journal* 94:772–87.

Tocqueville, A. de. 2004a. *Democracy in America.* New York: Library of America.

———. 2004b. *Oeuvres Complètes.* Vol. 3. Bibliothèque de la Pléiade. Paris, Gallimard.

Veyne, P. 1976. *Le Pain et le Cirque.* Paris, Seuil.

Watzlawick, P. 1978. *The Language of Change.* New York, Basic Books.

Wiener, J. 1998. "Managing the Iatrogenic Risks of Risk Management." *Risk: Health, Safety and Environment* 9:39–82.

Williams, B.A.O. 1981. "Internal and External Reasons." In idem, *Moral Luck: Philosophi-*

cal Papers, 1973–1980. Cambridge University Press.

Winter, S. 1964. "Economic 'Natural Selection' and the Theory of the Firm." *Yale Economic Essays* 4:225–72.

~ INAUGURAL LECTURES AT THE COLLÈGE DE FRANCE ~

This essay is a translation from the French of an inaugural lecture delivered at the Collège de France on June 1, 2006.

Since its foundation in 1530, the Collège de France has had as its principal mission to provide instruction, not in established disciplines of knowledge, but rather in "knowledge in the process of being made": in scientific and intellectual research itself. The lectures are open to everyone, free of charge, without registration, and do not lead to diplomas.

In accord with its motto (*Docet omnia*, "It teaches everything"), the Collège de France has fifty-two professorships covering a vast range of disciplines. In addition, every year chairs of European studies, international studies, artistic creation, and—starting in 2006—technological innovation are appointed.

The professors are chosen freely by their peers, in relation to the evolution of the sciences and knowledge. With the arrival of every new professor, a new chair is created that may either continue, at least in part, the heritage of an earlier chair, or open up a new area of teaching.

The first lecture given by a new professor is his inaugural lecture.

Given formally in the presence of his colleagues and a large audience, this lecture provides him with an opportunity to situate his work and his teaching in relation to that of his predecessors and to the most recent developments in research.

Thus the inaugural lectures not only sketch a picture of the state of our knowledge and thereby contribute to the history of each discipline, but also introduce us to the workshop of the scholar and researcher. Many of them have constituted, in their domains and in their time, significant and even resounding events.

They are addressed to a broad, enlightened audience seeking to improve its understanding of the evolution of contemporary science and intellectual life.

5